V O C E S 8

A CAPPELLA SONGBOOK

PETERS EDITION LTD

A member of the EDITION PETERS GROUP
FRANKFURT/M. · LEIPZIG · LONDON · NEW YORK

VOCES8 is managed by

ARTIST MANAGEMENT

Peters Edition Limited
2–6 Baches Street
London
N1 6DN
Tel: 020 7553 4000
Fax: 020 7490 4921
Email: sales@editionpeters.com
Internet: www.editionpeters.com

A. Goldsmith

CONTENTS

About the songs . . .

Feeling Good (Anthony Newley and Leslie Bricusse), arranged Jim Clements

George Michael . . . Muse . . . The Pussycat Dolls . . . all have covered this great song. We hope you like the VOCES8 version too! It was commissioned for a wedding that we sang at in our first year as a professional group. The venue was Winchester Cathedral, the acoustic wrapped itself around this fantastic melody and the music just took off. Now we sing this song on concert platforms all over the world. Make sure you really enjoy the last chord – it's a spine-tingling moment in any concert.

Nobody Does It Better (M. Hamlisch and C. Bayer-Sager), arranged Jim Clements

Wherever we travel in the world, we like to represent the very best of British... And what better British character can there be than James Bond? This song, from the film *The Spy Who Loved Me*, is the first of our Bond arrangements to be published, but anyone who has seen us in concert will know there are more to come. This song regularly gives Andrea, one of our fabulous sopranos, the chance to bring a dash of her 'Bond Girl' to the stage.

Folksong Medley, arranged Emily Dickens

This arrangement draws together a pair of stunningly emotive melodic lines from the Scottish and Irish folk traditions. The lower voices create a drone on which the tenor and upper voices explore the beautifully simple and instantly recognizable harmonies of these folk songs. This arrangement was first performed by VOCES8 on tour in the USA in 2011.

Erlkönig (Franz Schubert), arranged Jim Clements

'Erlkönig' tells the terrifying tale of a young boy and his father riding home through the forest and being chased by the Erl King. This arrangement of the famous Schubert song conveys a real sense of melodrama: each voice has a chance to inhabit the characters from the story while Schubert's original piano part is brought to life by the other voices. The piece is great fun – and a great challenge for anyone who likes to sing 'd-v-d' repeatedly, and very fast!

Shenandoah, arranged Thomas Hewitt Jones

This beautiful arrangement was made for VOCES8 by our composer-in-residence, Thomas Hewitt Jones, to celebrate the group's fifth anniversary. As part of the anniversary celebrations, VOCES8 toured the USA for two months in early 2012: a really special moment for the group came when we performed this song in the Shenandoah Valley itself.

Opera Medley, arranged Jim Clements

This is one of VOCES8's earliest arrangements, and one of our most popular arrangements worldwide. Many well-loved tunes from famous operas appear throughout the song, and for anyone who has seen this performed by VOCES8 on stage, you'll know that there's plenty of opportunity to bring the songs to life by unleashing your inner Diva! 'Opera Medley' was originally written for VOCES8 to perform at the Royal Opera House in London.

Wade in the Water, arranged Jim Clements

This famous spiritual is really brought to life in a new way by Jim's brilliant arrangement, and it's a song that we feel suits VOCES8 really well. Big writing, fantastic harmonies and a real joy of life burst out of every line. We hope you enjoying singing this as much as we do!

The Luckiest (Ben Folds), arranged Jim Clements

'The Luckiest' is the most frequently requested song in any VOCES8 workshop. A song that brings a tear to the eye of performers and listeners, this arrangement conjures with a powerful text and sweeping harmonies to produce real emotion and depth of feeling. This is a favourite of VOCES8 audiences, and we can't wait to hear other ensembles putting their voices to this song too.

Zu den Stücken . . .

Feeling Good (Anthony Newley und Leslie Bricusse), bearbeitet von Jim Clements

George Michael, Muse, die Pussycat Dolls – sie alle haben diesen großartigen Song gesungen. Wir hoffen, dass auch die Fassung von VOCES8 auf Anklang stößt! Sie entstand für eine Hochzeit, bei der wir im ersten Jahr unseres Bestehens als professionelles Ensemble singen durften. Sie fand in der Kathedrale von Winchester statt, wo die Musik – von der herrlichen Akustik des Raumes getragen – wunderbar zur Geltung kam. Inzwischen singen wir das Stück auf Konzertbühnen in aller Welt. Den Schlussakkord sollte man ausgiebig genießen – er ist bei jedem Konzert ein Gänsehaut-Moment.

Nobody Does It Better (M. Hamlisch und C. Bayer-Sager), bearbeitet von Jim Clements

Egal, wohin die Reise führt – stets versuchen wir, uns von unserer „britischen" Seite zu präsentieren. Und was könnte britischer sein als James Bond? Mit dem vorliegenden Song aus dem Film *Der Spion, der mich liebte* erscheint hier unser erstes Bond-Arrangement im Druck. Jeder, der uns schon einmal im Konzert erlebt hat, weiß jedoch, dass wir noch einige mehr auf Lager haben. Andrea – eine unserer fabelhaften Sopranistinnen – erhält mit diesem Stück immer wieder die Gelegenheit, ein wenig „Bond-Girl" zu spielen.

Folksong Medley, bearbeitet von Emily Dickens

Dieses Arrangement verbindet zwei stimmungsvolle und ergreifende Melodielinien, die der schottischen bzw. irischen Tradition entstammen. Die tiefen Stimmen erzeugen einen stetigen Bordun-Klang, über dem sich in Tenor und Oberstimmen die wunderbar eingängigen und charakteristischen Harmonien der beiden Volkslieder entfalten. Uraufgeführt wurde diese Bearbeitung von VOCES8 auf ihrer Konzertreise durch die USA im Jahr 2011.

Erlkönig (Franz Schubert), bearbeitet von Jim Clements

Die schaurige Geschichte des „Erlkönigs" handelt von Vater und Sohn, die nachts durch den Wald nach Hause reiten und vom Erlkönig verfolgt werden. Die vorliegende Bearbeitung des berühmten Schubert-Lieds bringt seine ganze Dramatik zum Ausdruck: Jede Stimme bekommt Gelegenheit, den Part einer der handelnden Personen zu übernehmen, während die übrigen Stimmen Schuberts Klavierbegleitung zum Leben erwecken. Ein Stück, das einfach Laune macht – und eine echte Herausforderung für alle, die unablässige und extrem schnelle „da-ba-das" lieben!

Shenandoah, bearbeitet von Thomas Hewitt Jones

Dieses phantastische Arrangement wurde von unserem „Composer in residence", Thomas Hewitt Jones, aus Anlass des fünfjährigen Bestehens von VOCES8 geschrieben: Zur Feier des Jubiläums unternahmen wir Anfang 2012 eine zweimonatige Konzertreise durch die USA. Die Aufführung des Songs vor Ort im Shenandoah Valley war ein überaus bewegender Moment für unser Ensemble.

Opera Medley, bearbeitet von Jim Clements

Dies ist eines der ersten Arrangements von VOCES8 – und weltweit eines unserer beliebtesten. Im Verlauf des Potpourris erklingen viele bekannte Melodien aus berühmten Opern, und alle, die das Stück bei einem VOCES8-Konzert auf der Bühne erlebt haben, wissen, dass es ausreichend Gelegenheit bietet, die Stücke lebendig werden zu lassen und die 'innere Diva' zu entfesseln! Ursprünglich wurde das „Opera Medley" für VOCES8 zur Aufführung am Londoner Opernhaus Covent Garden geschrieben.

Wade in the Water, bearbeitet von Jim Clements

Dieses berühmte Spiritual erstrahlt durch die großartige Bearbeitung von Jim Clements in ganz neuer Frische und passt nach unserem Empfinden besonders gut zu VOCES8. Jede einzelne Zeile sprüht nur so vor Klangfülle, grandiosen Harmonien und echter Lebensfreude. Wir hoffen, dass es anderen genauso viel Spaß macht wie uns, diesen Song zu singen!

The Luckiest (Ben Folds), bearbeitet von Jim Clements

„The Luckiest" ist das mit Abstand gefragteste Stück bei jedem VOCES8-Workshop. Der eindringliche Text und die getragenen Akkorde des vorliegenden Satzes rufen tiefe Ergriffenheit hervor, Sänger wie Zuhörer sind nicht selten zu Tränen berührt. Das Stück zählt daher zu den Publikumsfavoriten, und wir freuen uns nun darauf, den Song auch in der Interpretation anderer Ensembles zu hören.

Feeling Good

Leslie Bricusse & Anthony Newley
arranged for VOCES8
by Jim Clements

still ephemeral: never too loud!

meno mosso, a piacere

Nobody Does It Better

M. Hamlisch & C. Bayer-Sager
arr. Jim Clements

Folksong Medley

'My Lagan Love' and 'She Moved Through the Fair'

Trad. arr. Emily Dickens

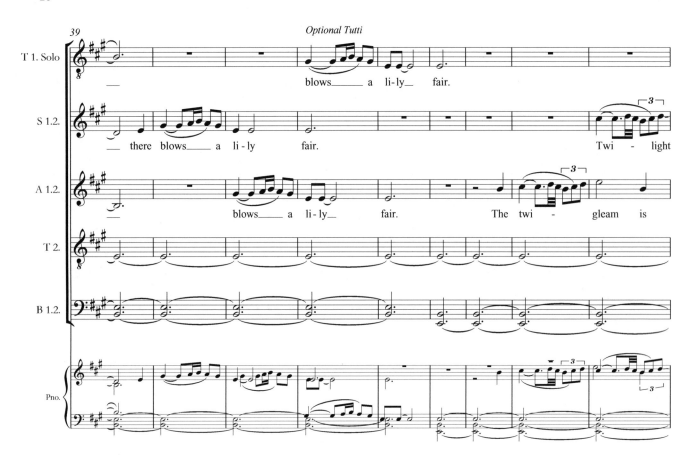

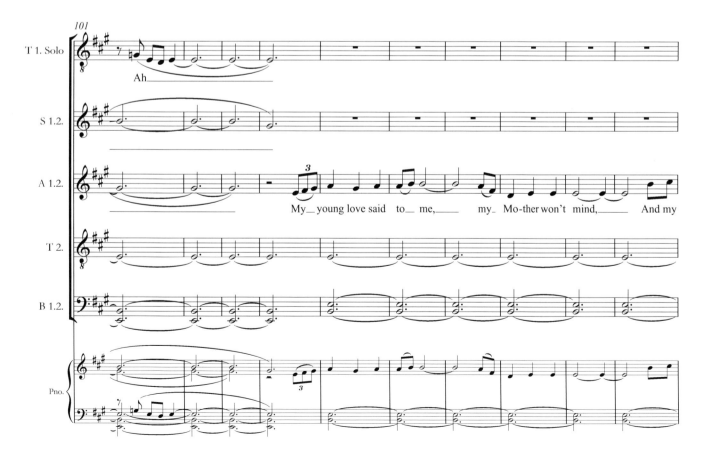

Erlkönig

Soprano 1 = 'The Narrator'
Alto 1 = 'The Boy'
Tenor 1 = 'The Alder/Elf King'
Bass 1 = 'The Father'

J.W. von Goethe

Franz Schubert
arranged for VOCES8
by Jim Clements

Shenandoah

American traditional
arranged for VOCES8
by Thomas Hewitt Jones

Shen-an- doah,___ I long to see you, A - way,___ I'mbound a - way,___ a-cross the

As the beginning but slightly slower, poignant, reminiscent

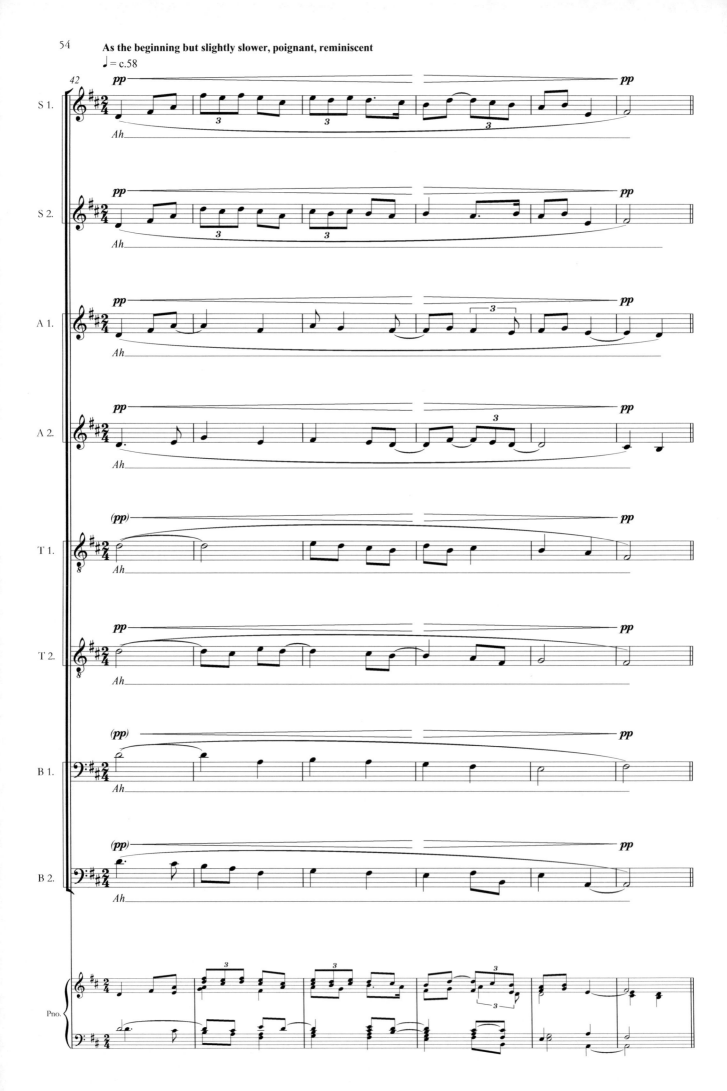

Opera Medley

Bizet/Mozart/Delibes/Verdi
arranged for VOCES8
by Jim Clements

Wade in the Water

Trad. Spiritual arranged for
Worcester Cathedral Chamber Choir
and adapted for VOCES8
by Jim Clements

64

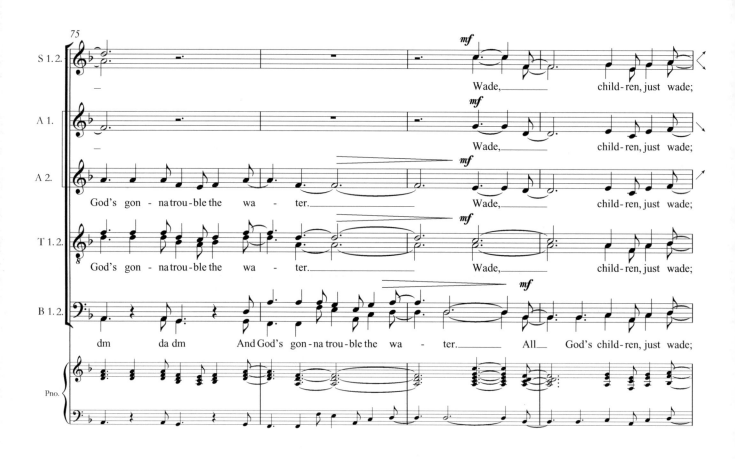

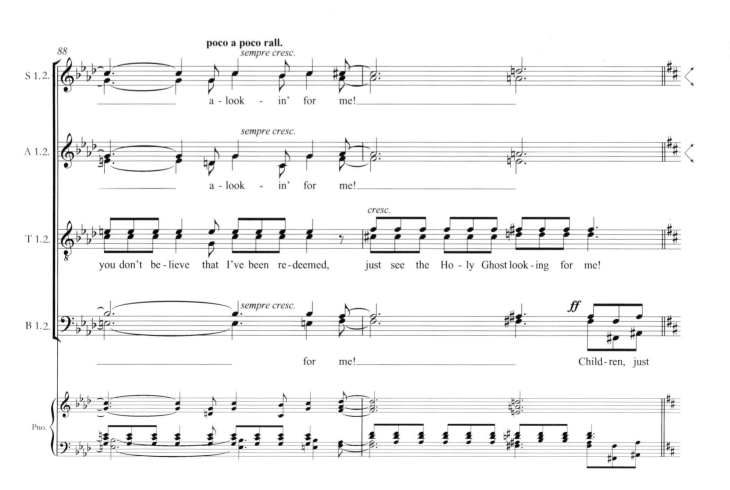

The Luckiest

Ben Folds
arranged for VOCES8
by Jim Clements